Strategic Growth in Inside Sales

How to Hire, Train, and Manage Your Inside Sales Team

Strategic Growth in Inside Sales

How to Hire, Train, and Manage Your Inside Sales Team

Dan Fowler

YouSpeakIt

PUBLISHING

The Easy Way to Get Your Book Done Right™

www.YouSpeakItPublishing.com

This book is dedicated to my wife, Jennifer, who has always believed in me with unwavering support and sacrifice. No one loves deeper than she.

Contents

Acknowledgments

This book has been inspired by the real events I have witnessed throughout my personal life and business career. I could not have written it without a number of special people. Thank you.

First, I want to thank Jesus, my Lord and Savior, for giving me the abilities, faith, and His continual leadership in my life to write this book.

Secondly, I want to thank my wife, Jennifer. When I need a thumb in my back, she provides one in the most tender and loving way. Thanks, Babe, I love you.

Thank you, Jenny Patterson, my personal coach, for your continual support in my coaching/consulting business by keeping me accountable to get this book written.

Thank you, Susan Smith, my business consultant, who always has my best interest in mind and repeatedly kept telling me, "you've *got* to write a book, you just *have* to."

Thank you, Chuck Polito, my business mentor, who always has the time and the ear to listen to me no matter the time or topic. A true lifelong friend.

Thank you, business owners and friends, who were an inspiration to me and provided both good and bad content in order to make the book realistic in today's business climate.

And a final thank you to YouSpeakIt Publishing, whose staff and personnel guided me through a process of writing this book from start to finish in a manner I fully trusted.

Introduction

How do you build a world-class inside sales team?

This guide offers you suggestions and solutions based on real-life experiences of business owners and sales executives within the business industry. This book will also help you develop realistic expectations for your business. There is another set of rules for inside sales reps that accept inbound calls, which we do not address in this book.

These guidelines and suggestions are for you if:

- Your company has an inside sales team that sets appointments for your outside territorial sales representatives or managers, or if the sales team sets appointments for the principal of the company, such as the president of a small business who is also the sales individual within that company.

- You are a business owner who does not have an outbound sales calling team, but you are thinking of building such a department.

- Your existing company is struggling with inside sales teams, and you are looking for practical help.

Many business owners and sales executives I've researched told me that managing the inside sales team is a big frustration that consumes much of their time and energy.

Before coming to us, their companies had tried different approaches, and each approach failed, such as hiring and managing their own staff, outsourcing, and contracting their inside sales teams to other sales organizations.

They just didn't know where to turn or what to do.

Moreover, they couldn't really be sure that the results reported by outside teams were accurate. A number of business owners I talked with said they had never seen results materialize in the way that they were promised. They expressed the wish that they had some type of manual or book they could consult to measure what they were doing.

So, I have written this book to be a guide for what to expect and how to sidestep potential problems, what I call *landmines*. Obviously, sidestepping some of the known problems allows you to reduce the amount of startup time and expenses. All business owners know that time is money; the old saying is correct.

Managers tend to read multiple books at a time, but the managers who are honest with themselves admit that they can take a principle from only one book at a time to another context.

I recommend reading this book all the way through, marking with a pencil or highlighter as you go. You'll also benefit from rereading and making notes in the margins. For the best results, you may wish to keep a piece of paper on hand and keep a running list of Action Steps or strategies you want to remember to try.

My hope is that you gain a concept of how important building an inside sales team is within your organization. This book will help you either build it from scratch or fine-tune what you currently have.

An inside sales team creates a great revenue stream. If you have an outside sales force making sales calls via influencers, associations, and referrals, that is not enough in today's marketplace. What you need is someone who can reach individuals you do not know who also have a need or know someone with a need. That particular need might not exist at that particular moment. I recommend a team that works on a continual basis and uses a continual touch program. Over a period of time, you might resurrect sales and potential appointments from those who, up front, have previously said no.

Time is of the essence. Revenue is vital to small- and medium-sized businesses. If following the guidance of this book decreases your time and effort of starting a sales team, then I have accomplished a major objective. I do not know every sales scenario that might develop. My disclosure is that this might not fit 100 percent into every company, but I have gained enough information and have had enough experience to know that you can tweak or modify these steps to meet the specific needs of your company.

I coach business managers to be *proactive* rather than *reactive*. You will have better results if you manage with what you can see and control, rather than simply hoping potential customers will dial in. As a business owner, I know it's better to be in control of your business, which is in part why you should employ an outbound-dialing inside sales team rather than not.

I hope you see the need to tap into an inside sales team. When you do so and follow the steps outlined in this book, you can build a business that is sustainable and repeatable for the good of yourself and for the people who work within your organization.

CHAPTER ONE

Hiring the Best Inside Sales Rep for Your Business

CULTURE FIT

Culture is a term used loosely within organizations to mean the environment of the workplace. It can be used to reference the core values of the company, how an employee fits in, or how it feels to work in the company. Like steel, the culture is tempered and shaped to form core values and the outcome of the company. It takes time to design the culture of your company; it won't happen over a weekend or over a matter of weeks.

Therefore, it's better to hire people first based on how you think they will fit in and add to the culture because you cannot teach culture to an individual. An individual brings it with them.

Culture is so important because it is the platform by which all the employees come together to build a successful company. Your company can follow the pathway to success only if everyone is going in the same direction — if everyone has the same tools and motivations. The fit between a potential team member and the culture of the company should be one of your primary considerations when hiring.

Guidelineswithintheculturecomefromyourcompany's core values: every thought and action contributed by the employee or management are guided through the core values, which are the definition of the company organization. Sometimes, it is best for the employees, along with management's blessing, to display the core values because the core values are how the employees are measured.

Hire First for Culture and Second for Skill

The problem of not hiring on culture, or hiring on skill alone, is that many individuals come into the organization with different levels of skillsets. At a successful company, skills within the company are on the same wavelength and skillsets intertwine. It's like a fabric that is woven together. You want them all to mesh together.

Let's imagine someone has agreed to take a job with your company not because they are well suited for the job, but simply for the sake of having a job. If their skillset is significantly higher or lower than the rest of the team, your culture will suffer because that individual will deteriorate the culture if they feel like they are overqualified or underqualified.

Skill is something that *can* be taught. Every position within a company has a unique skillset, something that needs to be defined. But you want to hire for suitability *and* skillset for a particular position. It must be a good match. Without a match between the skillset of the individual and the culture of the company, you could end up with a very capable employee, but their personality — how they collaborate and communicate with others — may not work with other members of the team. This difference in personalities can affect productivity.

Employee Interaction

An employee needs to engage with other individuals within the company. No one is an island. People working in isolation only deteriorate the culture of the company.

If an individual walks into their office, shuts the door, and remains there from 8:00–5:00 and doesn't even come out for lunch, that type of individual is basically saying: *I am not approachable. I am just here to do my job.*

The engagement and interaction between employees can be serious and humorous. You can laugh together. When each worker within the company interacts with another, a bond is formed. And those interactions increase productivity as people share their issues and problems, so they may work together for solutions with other individuals at their level or even at a management level. The interactions should be transparent. People can work with self-awareness and with the understanding that everyone is there to help. The workplace can become part of a family, and the family that plays together and works together is successful together. That is why you want to have engagement between all employees.

If you have a good culture, one employee can go to another and say frankly: *I did not receive the information you were going to forward to me, so I cannot be accountable for doing my part of the job.*

A good culture ensures you have checks and balances. Your employees feel comfortable enough with each other to address concerns up front. The interactions and the communication skills produce the right culture fit.

Holding the Core Values of the Company

Both management and employees need to hold to the core values of the company. The core values of the company should be visible and accessible so that everyone is pulling in the same direction. As mentioned earlier, it is best for them to be written down. Everything that is brought forward, whether it be a problem or a solution, should all be driven by what the core values of the company are. Any type of reward or accolade from one person to another should be given and addressed by referencing the core value the person exhibited.

This is important to the workers but also to the entire culture fit within the company itself. The core values should be so evident throughout the company that they exude from internal workings to external client relations, interactions, and the public face of the company.

Whether it's a message of value that the client has for you — *We love our clients!* or *Clients come first!* — it should be dominant enough in the culture of your company that clients will perceive it. If your core values are demonstrated by all the employees, your customers will notice and respond because of the way they are treated.

Although you hire for culture and you build a culture within a company, it's not just for internal purposes only; it's for your external client base, your vendor base, and your partner base. They also receive the benefits of having a great company with good employees who fit the culture.

When you hire to fit the culture, the personal values of the individual need to match the company's core values as well.

PERSONALITY FIT

The reason that you seek a personality fit is to reduce the potential for conflict within the company. As you consider hiring to match the culture fit, you also want to look to hire in order to match personalities. In a sense, you don't want everyone to be the same. You want them to have enough of a difference that they compensate for any weaknesses within the team. They can learn to cover for each other and form a good working bond.

Your newly hired worker needs to have a strong, flexible, and adaptable personality so that, again, they get along with everyone. They need to have an intuitive sense to hold the corporate mission and the values of the company within their character.

Attitude

Attitude makes a big difference in an employee. In the hiring process, you'll want to learn about their attitude.

Some questions to consider as you get to know them through interviewing:

- Are they coachable?
- Are they willing to learn?
- Are they creative?
- What type of ego do they have — is their attitude for themselves or for the company?
- What drives that attitude?
- Are they a team player?
- When you observe the overall attitude, do you think other workers would consider this person's attitude good or bad?

If their attitude needs to be held in check, this may not be the worker you want. You don't want to hire renegades who will run off and tear your company in half by doing their own thing.

Motivation

People are motivated by different things. Most people are motivated by money, by the almighty dollar. Although this is a good motivation, it's not necessarily the only one or the most important one. An individual I know makes a lot of money, made presidents' club in sales for three years straight, and makes a nice six-figure income. If you were to ask her if money is the motivator, she'd say no. It's really her passion, her intrinsic purpose, of helping people. She has the passion to take individuals from where they are into a better way of life. It's most important to her to help others better their lives, not to make a lot of money. She has learned the secret that by helping other people, you basically become successful because they in turn are motivated to help you.

> *Don't do this because you have to, but*
> *because you want to. Don't do it out of*
> *greed, but out of a desire to serve.*
> ~ 1 Peter 5:2 NOG

There are individuals who are motivated by success. There are different motivations for people based on where they are in their life. It can range according to age or their position or economic system.

Awareness

How do you know if someone is self-aware?

They are honest with themselves. They can look deep inside and perceive and describe their strengths and weaknesses. Knowing their strength, they won't use it to overpower others. They won't emphasize it to the point that it sticks out like a sore thumb. Understanding their weakness, they'll seek to become stronger through additional training.

Being self-aware starts by being transparent with yourself, which is a hard thing to do. You may recognize that you want to change something about yourself. Changing is hard. Sometimes, you can tackle changes yourself; other times, you'll need help from someone else.

The awareness of strengths and weaknesses is crucial to achieve success, any goal, or target. The key to self-awareness is being willing to acknowledge where you need growth or change within yourself. We all need help. We all have a weakness. Sometimes we don't want to say that we do, but we do. The most successful people are willing to improve their weaknesses and hone their strengths as well.

ASSESSMENT TOOLS

Assessment tools are valuable in the business world today for measuring or identifying different personality traits, motivators, and desires. They also focus on the individual as a whole being. By using different assessment tools, you can gather a more complete picture of the individual, which is what you as a manager or owner of a company want to know. If you know the whole individual, then you know with confidence that you are hiring someone who fits inside your culture, will be a good personality fit for your company, and will help drive the success and the productivity of the company.

You would not want to look at only half a Monet painting because it wouldn't mean anything to you. If you look at the whole picture, you understand the beauty of it and what it represents, with all its intricacies and designs. Assessment tools can bring that information of the whole picture forward so you can make a knowledgeable and intelligent decision as to whether to hire this individual.

Interviewing Techniques, Including Role-Playing

One of the major interviewing techniques is role-playing. For example, a common role-play interview technique is to select a common item such as a pen or baseball glove that the candidate must sell to the interviewer.

Role-playing tells you so many things about the candidate on the other side of the desk. A role-play gives you a sense of how this person is going to speak and act in front of others. You watch their body language, eye contact, and how they maneuver.

Another interview technique is *dialing a white list*. The inside sales candidate cold-calls ten to fifteen clients using a script. First, give the person a certain amount of time to review the script. Then, have them pick up the phone, punch in the numbers, and use the script with the new clients.

Once I interviewed a person with great credentials. He had been doing inside calling and appointment-setting calls for more than ten years. We gave him a script to review. We came back five minutes later and asked him if he had command of the script. He felt he did.

I handed him a list of ten potential clients and said, "These are the phone numbers and the names you are going to call. Follow the script. If they ask you any questions, use these." I showed him handouts he could refer to in case some common questions came up. He was in a small conference room, a safe environment.

Within three telephone calls, I knew he was not the right individual. He came in with credentials as if he was a five-star general. But in action, the way he handled those calls was more like a private.

These two, role-playing and dialing the white list, are two great interviewing techniques.

Industry Standard Tests

Of the three methods, this is the one I really struggle with because I know there are so many types of assessment tests that are on the market. The ones that seem to be the most popular are the Myers Briggs Type Indicator and the DISC profile. I recommend these. They give you a good sense of the candidate's personality and character and how they'll fit into your organization.

Giving the test is just one part of the process. You also need to read the test and analyze the results to learn whether what you are reading about that individual is a good fit for your company.

Third-Party Approval

Third-party approval comes from other people in the organization who are going to come into contact with that individual. It might be the operations manager or someone within operations. It could be someone within HR; it typically is. It could be on the sales development side of the company. Therefore, the third-party opinions should be considered.

Have a number of interviews with the prospect, rather than just one or two. Have people in different positions, such as the Chief Operating Officer or the owner of the company, interview them. Ask the interviewers to follow the same script with the same questions for each candidate so that after the candidate is dismissed, they may compare candidates on equal ground.

By having the same questions, your interviewers can compare the candidate's high and low points based on the same answer. Those reports must be shared with the ownership of the company. Interviewing can be done internally or by a recruitment firm.

You may even wish to have a team of six people doing the interviewing: three from inside the company, and three from another company or a recruiting firm. A recruiting company is trained in asking the right questions for hiring, whereas within the business, your primary concern is whether the candidate is a good fit within the organization.

You start with the basic questions of how, why, and whom would I want to hire for this position?

Questions your team can consider are:

- Is this candidate suitable for the position?
- Do they have a behavioral alignment within the company?
- What does their body language communicate about them?
- Are they well-spoken, or do they stutter and pause?
- Do they seem like they are unsure of themselves?
- Are they willing to push forward gently, or do they seem aggressive?

Another great reason to include different inputs in the interviewing process is to look for and discuss the stress level of that individual. How stressed they are will be a key indicator of their personality. Stress within an organization will destroy an organization. If someone is overly stressed, they will not produce efficiently. Including several interviewers will contribute to creating a whole picture of the individual.

Internal interviewers will have a good sense of the core values and the type of culture within the company. It will be easy for them to decide whether the candidate is a good fit. There are different types of results that will come through different interviewers.

CHAPTER TWO

CHAPTER TWO

Training a Successful Inside Sales Rep

ESTABLISH A TRAINING SCHEDULE

An inside representative sets the appointment with a decision-maker or prospect and the outside sales rep attends the meeting. The outside sales rep shows the prospect exactly how your company can provide a service or product that addresses some need — perhaps an area of discomfort or pain, or a problem that needs to be fixed.

Your best chance at successfully training your inside sales rep (ISR) is to set a schedule. Training is a process that needs to be followed from Point A to Point B. It will most likely take longer than you'd normally think for new hires to become proficient. You want to tighten the schedule enough to use time efficiently yet relax it enough to allow the time needed to create success.

Training Takes Time

From the first step of hiring a sales rep to the point when they become productive could take as long as six months. A lot of managers and business owners feel that it's a process that they can rush, that they can just throw things at the ISRs and they will learn on their own time. It typically takes between two and four weeks from the time you train an ISR to have them set their first appointment.

Let's say you hire your ISR in January. During March, April, and May, they are going to be gaining skills little by little by little, such as learning the phone script and setting appointments. They will absorb information that is needed to work independently and productively. By *productive,* I mean they can gain the trust of the prospect and make them feel comfortable enough during the call to set up appointments for the outside sales team to follow up on.

Within this training period, you need to not overburden the inside sales rep. A better way to think of this is to *make it fun.* Many training sessions involve sitting in a chair for eight hours a day listening to tapes. I know of someone who fell asleep their first hour into training! Obviously, this is not a situation you want. Just remember: slow is fast. There are no shortcuts. Take the time to confirm your rep is 100 percent fully trained. Give them the time to go at their own speed to gain competency.

In addition to taking the time required to do a good job with the training, other factors might interrupt the time frame, such as vacations, holidays, or life issues. Allow more time than you think you'll need because you will need it.

Prepare a Roadmap

In addition to considering a timeline, your training program requires a roadmap that includes the equipment and materials the rep will need and an end goal for success.

For equipment, you'll need:

- Personal computer
- Phone system
- Customer Relations Management (CRM) software
- Call scripts
- Email templates

To teach your trainee how to follow the scripts, you can make use of shadowing – in which a new rep follows and observes an experienced rep – and instructional videos. Another method is for the inside sales rep to shadow an outside sales rep at an appointment that the inside sales rep has scheduled.

You'll need to schedule time for meetings along the way to offer feedback and discuss questions or issues that may have come up for the trainee. You'll also need to factor in how and when to monitor their activities to assess how they're doing.

Your road map should include peer groups and webinars with other individuals in the same position who can give the ISR feedback. These are great ways to support a new rep.

Always keep the end goal in mind. The end goal will guide the process in the best way to bring the new rep success. If your new rep is successful, the business will be successful.

Deadlines

At what point will you expect your new rep to be competent?

You need to install a realistic time frame that covers all the training issues and the process. Put the timeframe on a calendar that is also visible to management and the inside sales rep themselves.

The deadline will be predicated on your business cycle and the information you expect your trainee to comprehend and integrate. Training is an ongoing operation and a process. Training never stops;

however, there needs to be a definite time by which the individual is competent and you are confident that they can start making the calls independently in a professional manner.

Let the inside sales rep know that once they have achieved the goal of competency within the designed timeframe, their compensation will reflect that. Monetary value is part of what drives the inside sales rep.

ESTABLISH A TRAINING PROCESS

There is so much within the training process itself. Your process is driven by the needs of your company, and you design it guided by your core values. Once you've developed the basic process, you can add to it to enrich it, or remove parts you feel may have diluted it, but you must start with a structure to take you from Point A to Point B.

In essence, it needs to be a step-by-step process with measurable goals and a visible and communicated goal at the end.

Training Step by Step

Your training program needs to be unified. Even with individual adaptations for the people you are training, it should follow a sequence and be consistent. As I mentioned before, you can add or delete from the basic format, but the process needs to be uniform.

You start by setting up a schedule. Include the number of training sessions or classes and the content taught in each session. Remember the way in which the content is taught should also be consistent.

Next, think about how you will build in time for evaluation. This is time for the ISR to give feedback on how the process is going for them and to ask questions. It is also for you to assess their progress. You could break it down evenly into a daily routine, such as a fifteen-minute check-in, or it could be a weekly meeting.

Follow a step-by-step procedure with built-in assessment. This way, your rep will know that by the time they finish the last step, they will have completed the training process and have everything they need to be successful.

Training Must Have a Measurable Objective

Peter Drucker, who is credited with inventing modern business management, gave the business world this quote, "If you cannot measure it, you can't improve it."

The measurable objectives for the training process boils down to what I call *key performance indicators*

(KPI). These are typically statistics that show how the program is running, how the ISR is acclimating to the process, and whether they comprehend the type of training process you use.

KPIs include:

- Number of outbound calls ISRs have made
- Number of conversations they have had with decision makers
- Number of appointments they've set
- Number of follow-up appointments they've set

The most obvious statistic to track is whether the call and conversation lead to a new business contract.

You can use forms to document the progress so both the management and the inside sales rep know that the step-by-step process is being fulfilled.

Another measurable outcome is whether you're getting a good return on your investment in training. One way to tell is to look at the prospect list the ISRs are creating from information gathered during the calls.

All those numbers together give you an indication of the success of your training program. If it's not as successful as you want, you can go back and fine tune or improve the training process. But you cannot do that unless you have the numbers because the numbers don't lie.

Training Must Be Followed in Order

There is a story about Vince Lombardi, the successful coach of the professional football team the Green Bay Packers. When he first addressed his team at the beginning of their training session each year, he would walk in and hold up a football and say, "Gentlemen, this is a football."

Even though this was obvious and elementary, Coach Lombardi would always start at the beginning. Likewise, Johnny Wooten, the legendary basketball coach for UCLA who won so many national titles with his basketball team, would open each season's training by telling all the players to bend down and tie their shoes. If their shoes were to come untied in the middle of a game, they might slip or trip and give up the ball, which could give points to the other team.

As elementary as these first steps are in these examples, they represent a systematic approach that needs to be done in each new beginning. From there, you can build confidently, block by block, like a pyramid or any building. You build the foundation first, and then you layer on top of that solid base. That is the approach that needs to be taken.

In the same way, you need to develop a rhythm or cadence for calls that the ISR can follow. How well they follow that cadence governs whether they can secure an appointment, which secures the outside sales rep sales call, which then secures the close. It's important that in following the order of the training process, they go step by step by step, no matter how elementary it might seem.

PROVIDE PROPER TRAINING TOOLS

To build anything successfully—whether it's a little paper airplane, the Great Sphinx of Giza, or the Eiffel Tower, you need tools. You must use the proper tools to fashion and mold your design. It's the same with the training process for inside salespeople. You need to put into their hands the proper training and tools to create a masterpiece, if you will. Even the Great Masters, such as Da Vinci and Rembrandt, had to have a good brush in hand to paint their masterpieces. For your inside salespeople to paint their masterpieces, they need to have the proper training tools to be successful.

Provide the Latest Technology

We live in a world where technology changes every day. For the inside salespeople to be successful, they need to have the latest technology. If they are competing against other companies that have the latest technology, you'd be leaving your crew behind if you did not give them the proper, most up-to-date tools.

As mentioned before, a few tools are essential. The first is the **telephone**.

In addition to allowing you to talk, the phone should include these features:

- Auto dialer
- Recording technology
- Playback feature
- Headsets to allow getting up and moving around

You will want your ISRs to have the right technology to do the job in the moment and to review the conversation so they can reflect on how they have performed.

The ISRs also need the latest **laptops** or **PCs** on which the latest version of application software and operating systems are installed.

They need the most current **customer relations management software (CRM)**. Outdated information is bad information. It won't provide success and it will be a waste of money. Be sure to update the software regularly.

Tools Must Be Easy to Use

Providing the right tools for the job means your ISRs will be more efficient. One of the characteristics of the right tools is that they make it possible for any individual with competence to learn how to use them.

In the example of an auto dialer, the ISR can make more calls per hour, which would, in essence, mean more conversations, which would mean more appointments, which in turn would gain more sales by experiencing ease of use on their telephone.

The same logic applies to the CRM or the calling device. During the call, the sales rep can simply add new contact information into the prospect list which can be used in future conversations. Later, the software automatically shows the prospect's contact info so the rep doesn't have to look it up mid-call. The prospect list can also track activity. It alerts the rep if there is any task that needs to be performed. There's also a way to record notes about the conversation to refer to. It brings forward any emails or cards.

Time is money when you are cold-calling prospects. With easy and efficient access to all that information, your inside sales rep will be highly productive and professional.

Great Tools Benefit Other Areas of the Process

Now that all the information is accessible, it's possible to bring those data to other areas of the process. The rep can build an internal prospect list or CRM of their own.

Who is your target client?

Are they in a certain niche or a different industry?

The CRM software should be flexible enough to take certain data, break it out into individual information, and custom build a more detailed customer profile. You can develop and break out the data, then massage and use it internally to build more detailed customer information. You can use that information to customize the call, which will increase your ability to retain customers. Referring to this info, the ISR can make use of these details to call the prospect by name. There's no better way to catch someone's attention than to call them by name.

If you call L.L.Bean, the clothier, and you are a part of their client base, they don't answer the phone with "Hello," they say, "Hello, Mr. or Ms. . . ." whatever your name is.

This is the kind of interface you want between your company, the rep, and your clients. The triangle of those three things—your company, the insides sales rep, and the potential client—builds a successful structure.

You want to take the information you have and build an internal prospect list that you can use for new customers or to retain the existing customers. Once the inside sales rep has that information, that process generates greater productivity, greater revenue, and greater sales.

CHAPTER THREE

The Roles and Responsibilities of an Inside Sales Rep

PERSONAL ATTRIBUTES

There are certain attributes that an inside sales rep must exhibit. These attributes create a healthy environment within the company and a positive work flow both for individual reps and the organization. The ISR who possesses these personal attributes experiences a sense of freedom and a clarity of mind. They function and perform in an individual way that is true to themselves.

When an ISR works authentically, the prospect perceives that the rep is transparent and honest. If the rep has transparency and honesty as part of their goals, you can rely on them to report back to the company exactly what has been said, according to the contract.

Self-Confidence

Self-confidence is often an overrated characteristic for a sales rep. But an ISR who exhibits healthy self-confidence is an individual who can perform at a high level. They tend to visualize what the outcome is going to be not only for the day or for the month, but even for the year. There is no fear of failure because they have confidence, drive, and a plan in place that they know will succeed. They proceed without doubt because they know the process. They trust in the process. They know that the process is going to deliver good results.

An attitude of self-confidence allows them to walk into the office each day. Their confidence fosters a proactive attitude of looking forward to the next dial, to make the next phone call, to talk to the next client, to handle whatever is given to them. The self-confidence that they have allows them to manage the situation, but more importantly, they feel like they are successful no matter the outcome of the situation.

Fearlessness of *No*

Most people fear hearing the word *no*. They take it personally, as a sign of failure or rejection. To succeed, however, you cannot fear that word. In fact, the sooner you hear that word, the better. The sooner in the process that the prospect lets you know they are at a no, the sooner you can change your strategy to move them toward a *yes*.

People who are not afraid of hearing *no* will be the most successful salespeople within the organization. First of all, they understand that no one can win them all.

Og Mandino, author of *The Greatest Salesman in the World,* says, "No one wins them all. And your failures, when they happen, are just part of your growth."

If you expect that you are going to receive *nos,* then when you receive a *yes,* it is all the better. There is a saying in sales: *If it takes ninety-nine nos out of a hundred to get one yes – which is a 99 percent failure rate – it might seem like a failure. However, it's not, because that one yes might be the deal of the century.*

Hearing no is a part of the game, part of what happens. Even if someone says no or says they have no interest, things can change. Good salespeople realize that even if the person on the other end of the phone says no, that's still a success—because that prospect picked up and answered the phone. With persistence, your inside sales rep can build on this small success to turn the early no into a bigger yes and a bigger deal for the company later. We'll talk more about persistence later in Chapter Three.

My nephew was a struggling college graduate. He joined the company as an inside sales rep who made cold calls looking for new business. He made so many dials a day, and he was rejected with so many *nos* that his mother tried talking him out of the job. She tried to have him find a new job. She was projecting herself onto him, thinking of what it must feel like to hear *no thank you* all day. But he was not daunted.

My nephew is now a manager and a trainer of this company, training the existing inside sales reps to be more successful. He is such a success that not only has he been promoted twice, but he also recently bought a fairly large and expensive car. He traded his 1980 car for a 2015 luxury car. He travels to different states for the company. It all started by being an inside sales rep who heard no for 99 percent of his calls.

To summarize, the rep should have no fear of *no*. When an inside sales rep is making a cold call, they are going to receive a no on the other side of the phone 99 percent of the time. But it's the persistence of the continual dialing and not settling for being rejected by hearing a number of *nos* that leads to that one yes.

That one yes is a success that could be the next appointment and deal that turns into revenue for the company. Even though someone hears the word no, all that tells them is *I'm not ready to buy yet*, but by persisting and consistently calling prospects on a regular basis, you will turn more of those *nos* into *yesses*.

Willingness to Succeed

Everyone feels like they want to be a success, but there are certain attributes that make you be a success. One of them is the willingness to do so.

Willingness to succeed means the ISR is willing to:

- Go the extra mile

- Focus on the job: the place, situation, customer, and the prospect the ISR is working with, the script

- Have the determination to succeed, no matter the obstacle, even if working ten-to-twelve-hour days

When you're willing to succeed, you don't stop. Once you find success, your willingness to succeed further compounds itself to expand and achieve greater success.

Willingness includes being proactive. The rep needs to take on whatever is necessary to train and educate themselves so that they never become stagnant. The willingness of the ISR to take time to educate themselves will lead to greater success.

To go the extra mile over the course of one year could mean making one more dial every day. If you take twenty working days in a month and you make one extra dial, that would be twenty times twelve months in a year, which would be two hundred forty more calls. If your closing rate is 10 percent, you have just increased the number of appointments, even though it is only 2.4 for that year. An increase of 2.4 appointments per year could mean a big gain in revenue for the company. The willingness to succeed might mean just one more call per day.

PERFORMANCE FLOW

The *performance flow* deals with how the inside sales rep performs on a day-to-day basis. Everything is tied to their performance, yet there needs to be a flow about it. A flow means it proceeds smoothly, like water out of a faucet, like a river flowing down to the sea. Nobody even thinks about it.

Three areas that enhance performance flow are:

1. Target setting
2. Prospect engagement
3. Script flexibility

There are many areas that we could discuss, but these are the three key areas I would like to address.

Target Setting

For the inside sales rep to become successful, they need to have a target number to strive for. Once the ISR has this target, their first action should be to break the number down into attainable numbers by the month, week, and day. An example would be if the target number of calls in a year is 12,000. The ISR can then figure that they need to make 1,000 calls a month, 250 calls a week, 50 calls a day.

Setting targets doesn't apply to business targets alone. Encourage your inside sales reps to make a chart with two columns. Instruct them to label one side *Business* and the other, *Personal*. Setting targets for the business and company *is* important, but they need to set personal targets as well to create a balanced life.

Business targets could include:

- Number of dials to make each day
- Number of conversations
- Percentage of conversations to the dials
- Number of appointments
- Percentage of appointments to schedule based on the number of conversations

Personal targets include:

- Income
- Social goals
- Self-worth

The first target should be: what is the **target income** that an inside sales rep wants to make?

Guide your ISR to use the numbers they recorded on the business side of their goals — the dials, conversations, and appointments, or the closure rate of each appointment — to figure what is the dollar amount of their average sale. Now, divide the income they want to obtain by their average income per sale, whether they are paid by full commission or commission on top of salary. This is the number of sales they need to hit in order to achieve their target income.

Target income ÷ average sale income = number of sales to achieve

The income target is probably the first target an inside sales rep would want to meet.

The **social target** reflects what the ISR feels is necessary to be considered a success in the eyes of their peers or within the company. Are they able to buy the things they have always wanted to own?

The **self-worth target** considers what it would take to match an individual's sense of self-worth. What would they have to obtain, what target income would they need to make so they believe the job is worth their time and effort?

Those are the targets that need to be set, both business and personal. They need to be measured and calculated daily so that the rep can know at a moment's notice if they are making their goal or not.

Prospect Engagement

Engaging prospects is one of the major keys to success for an inside sales rep. Once the prospect is on the phone, the rep has only five seconds before they determine whether they want to continue speaking to the rep.

What is it within that first five seconds that is going to make them decide whether they hang up, tell the rep that they are not interested, or ask the rep to continue speaking with them?

We will go into this in the next section, which focuses on scripts and how to gain prospects' attention within that five seconds.

But once the rep has the prospect on the line, how can the rep keep them engaged?

The rep wants to engage with clients on a periodic basis, even after the first phone call, speaking with them about what they want to speak about. The prospect might answer and not want to talk about business, and the rep might ask them how their day is. The rep and prospect could go into a personal conversation, in which they never talk business. But, the rep is skillfully talking to them about what the prospect wants to talk about because they have experienced something that could have happened two minutes before the ISR got them on the telephone call. The success in talking with new prospects lies in the ability to be present with them. Listening to what they say, a successful rep learns to go where the client leads the conversation.

Once that conversation is concluded and the rep has ended the call, the rep can follow up with the second part of engagement in a variety of ways:

- Write a letter or notecard that says you've been thinking about what they said and offer a resource to them.
- Send them a newsletter from the company.
- Email them a link to an informative, topical blog.
- Connect with the prospect on social media.
- Send them a gift.

As far as gifts go, sending a gift card is a simple way to show appreciation. A gift card from an inside sales rep communicates: *I am thinking about you. If you ever have a question or need to talk to me about my service, please give me a call.*

You could keep them engaged with an announcement — something regarding your company or their company. Once you have learned and listened to what they want to talk about, conversing with them on that particular subject, the prospect will continue to accept future phone calls from the ISR. With this kind of relationship, even if they say *No, we're not ready* up front or on the back end, you can have confidence that they likely will do business with you. You are developing their trust.

Script Flexibility

The inside sales rep should always have and follow a script.

Although it may be tempting for the rep to respond more spontaneously to the conversation and improvise, this presents a problem. If they were successful in creating a sale, when they improvise they have no record of how they got to the sale. If they try to retrace steps to recreate a successful call, they're lost. Using a script means they can trace their steps without losing valuable time.

It's better to stick to the script while staying flexible. The script will provide you a solid, repeatable base, and the flexibility will allow you to follow wherever the prospect takes you. With practice, the sales rep learns to balance these two abilities.

There is an old agent term, *waymark,* that refers to a marker along a path that guided travelers walking from city to city. By seeing that marker, often a stake in the ground, they knew they were on the right path. Each inside sales rep needs to have waymarks, if you will, in their script, so when they depart from it to engage with the prospect, they can find their way back.

> *Set up road signs; put up guideposts.*
> *Take note of the highway, the road that you take.*
> ~ Jeremiah 31:21 NIV

A good signal to find the waymark is when the potential client says: *Can you tell me more about your services?*

Although a script needs to be closely followed, the inside sales rep needs to have the flexibility and wisdom to go off script. Using the waymarks, they also need to come back to the script to meet their objective: gaining the appointment.

POSITIVE RESULTS

There are three primary indicators of positive results. I've learned through experience that if the inside sales reps target these three attributes, they will experience better outcomes.

It's Not All About the Numbers

The rep's numbers are important measurements of success. There are other factors that are just as important as numbers. In addition to *quantity,* the inside sales representative needs to consider *quality.* A lower number of dials and conversations is not necessarily a negative outcome if the leads and appointments build a better-quality lead that in the long term will benefit the revenue of the company. That is really what we are going to be looking at: how to create higher quality.

The inside sales rep needs to build relationships. An inside sales rep may be assigned to make a call every five minutes. Instead, they spend ten to fifteen minutes building a relationship with a prospect. It's true that they could have made three phone calls during that fifteen-minute time frame, but building the relationship is more important. The rep may not obtain a target number of fifty calls a day, but if they make better-quality calls, in the long run, they will be more productive with thirty-three calls than with fifty. By building relationships, the ISR is building trust that, down the road, is more likely to lead to more sales.

Right Timing

Timing is another important factor in assessing the success of the inside sales rep's calls. Calling at a convenient time for the prospect means that the rep is not being a pest, not making the prospect feel that they are being chased down or hunted. Therefore, even if the rep dials only once a week, if the timing is perfect, it's still a success.

My research has shown that calls made on Tuesdays, Wednesdays, and Thursdays show a higher degree of success than the week bookend-days of Monday and Friday. However, calls made after four o'clock on a Monday afternoon or after three o'clock on a Friday afternoon achieve almost the same degree of success. On a personal note, my largest sale was made with a phone call after six o'clock in the evening.

Deep Conversations

A major success of an inside sales rep is building a deep conversation with the prospect. If they want to talk about their kids, their dog, their feelings, their family, their favorite sports team, or the weather, it doesn't make a difference. The rep talks with the prospect about any area of interest they bring up and finds a way through that topic back to their waymark in the script. They stay connected to the prospect by way of the prospect's interests.

Being up to date on current events will keep the prospect engaged in a conversation by asking good, open-ended questions. By keeping the conversation relevant, and being present, the ISR could engage the prospect in conversation for as long as they'd like. Obviously, they do not want to waste their own time nor the prospects, but the deeper they can go in the conversation, the more successful they'll be.

After a great conversation, the rep will want to create a record of the conversation, using one of these methods:

- Audio recording
- Written notes added to the prospect list
- Notes added to the CRM

A successful ISR writes important notes down and puts them somewhere retrievable to refer to those same notes during the next call with that person. When the rep is able to reach the prospect a second time, the conversation doesn't have to start at the shallow level. They can pick up where they left off last time, going to a deeper level. This helps the prospect feel cared for and attended to. The rep builds trust. People will buy and set appointments from inside sales reps whom they trust and feel care about them.

I know how I feel. If someone calls me and they start the conversation with, *Hey, Dan, last time you were talking about one of your kids being sick. Are they okay?* It's a totally different conversation than when another rep calls me not knowing anything about me or my business.

Persistence

The art of persistence has been lost. There are so many alternatives that divert our attention; if we fail in one place, we can simply try another option.

For the inside sales person, persistence is an indispensable quality.

The ISR must dial a number, even when everything inside their body and their mind is saying: *It's no use. I am not going to get that person. He is going to tell me no again. He is going to hang up on me again. He blew me off before. I was embarrassed last time. I shouldn't even be dialing this guy because it just doesn't make sense for me to do it.*

A sales rep needs to have the persistence to say: *I am going to do it! I am in the process. I am totally committed to success, and I am willing to succeed. I can take another no. I am going to dial this guy again.*

When I go on sales calls, I like to ask why the person has decided to take the appointment.

There is a percentage of those prospects who look at me and say, not that it's because they wanted to hear what I had to say, or that they think our product is great and they're ready to buy, but: *Your inside sales rep was pretty persistent. After a while, I started to believe you must be selling something good because she keeps calling me. I took the appointment just so she would get off my back.*

An inside sales representative dialed a new company five times. Each time that she was connected to the President of the company, he did not even let her finish her script or her introduction. He just hung up on her.

It wasn't until she phoned him the sixth time that he picked up the phone and said, "I was just testing you to see what your persistence level would be. How can I help you?"

Persistence is so key to success for a rep. I like to conclude with this true story. It's an example from my own life. It's a story that took place over a year, almost two years. My inside sales rep set an appointment for me. I signed in to the office, gave the receptionist my name and why I was there. The individual I was going to see was a top executive of the company. The receptionist came back and told me that he did not have time for me.

I went back out to the car, called my inside sales rep, and said, "He blew me off. He was here, but he did not see me. Can you try to reschedule the appointment?"

It took her roughly six months before she was able to reschedule the appointment. I went back to the same building I'd gone to before, walked up to the same receptionist, signed in like I had done before, and gave her my business card.

She walked to the back of the office and returned about a minute later and said, "He's tied up. He can't see you."

I took my business card back, walked out to my car, called my sales rep, and said, "He blew me off again. He was here. He saw my card, but he didn't take the appointment. Try to reschedule it."

About six months after the second attempt to see the executive, the ISR called me and said, "You remember so-and-so? Well, I scheduled another appointment with him, but I said I would have you call him before you leave your office."

Being as stubborn as I am as an outside sales rep, and since I was going to be in the area anyway, I decided to go and make the sales call. The sales call was not with the executive who had turned me down twice before. It was with two other individuals of that same company without an executive title. I met with them and took an hour and a half to introduce our services to them.

Four months after I met with those two individuals, I was in front of the executive, and he signed our contractual agreement. The reason he didn't meet with me the previous two times was that the company was going through some turbulent times. The old president was selling the company, and this executive was one of a group who were buying the company. That is why he did not want to see me at those earlier times.

The contract he signed for this one deal was for as much as our company had done in the previous year. My inside sales representative's persistence with this one customer increased my company's growth from the previous year to the current year by 100 percent. And, she was paid very well. She earned it.

CHAPTER FOUR

Measuring the Results of Your Inside Sales Rep

SET YOUR GOALS

I know that the words *goals* and *targets* are overused. But the bottom line is that you need to have something precise that you can point to. Remember, nothing measured means nothing gained. Considering these factors, you as a business owner will have a better handle on whether a particular rep is working well within your culture. By the end of the assessment process, you will see whether your company, your reps, and you are the most productive you can be.

Methods for Exceeding Goals

Your goals for the ISRs should be aligned within the company's annual goals for reaching the projected revenue. That means you must figure out what the company's needs are to be profitable. After all, that is why the company is in business: to be profitable.

Once you have determined that revenue number, the goals can be divided among individual inside sales reps. When you have communicated that number to the inside sales reps, they must agree to take responsibility for their percentage of the company's revenue—no distraction from the left or the right. They must apply *the peanut philosophy.*

The peanut philosophy is this: Your inside sales rep is standing in line with other inside sales reps. On the floor in front of them is a peanut they must push with their nose across a finish line. The gun goes off, and the inside sales rep focuses on their own peanut—which in this analogy would be the goal—and pushes it down the floor without looking to the right or the left to see how his competitors are doing. The one who doesn't waste time or attention checking out what else is happening, the one who holds a singular focus, will win the race. They will meet their target number.

Is the inside sales rep capable of reaching the target?

As an example, let's say you've figured out that each rep needs to bring in $45,000 for the year. One rep has only made $30,000 in the past. In my experience, the reps who have not hit a certain income level or threshold will not meet your current income sales expectations. Unless you see a real desire to achieve in that person, do not continue to invest time or effort into their success.

You Must Follow a Process

In Chapter Two, I emphasized the importance of a process in training your reps. The same is true of helping each of your reps meet their goals. You need to define what that process will look like. Then, the inside sales rep must stay within the process.

I recently drove through the mountains of Utah and Colorado. There were treacherous curves, hairpin turns, and at times, sheer cliffs on each side of the road. The slightest mistake would have led to a deadly crash if I had gone over the line. Around each curve, there was a guardrail to guide me. The guardrails kept me from going off course and helped guide me safely to my destination. The guardrails of your process must be around every turn for your reps.

Can the inside sales reps stay within the guardrails?

This analogy leads me to another step regarding the ability to follow a process. As I was twisting and turning around those mountains, there were times I had to slow down, and there were other times I had to speed up. How the ISR manages time is another area that can be measured.

There will be times when the inside sales rep will have to slow down the process to properly navigate an appointment or a deal. A skilled inside sales rep knows to slow down to meet the timing of the prospect they are speaking with and to speed up when they realize that the prospect is not ready to make a decision. They need to know when it is better to move to the next call. The inside sales rep's time management is definitely a self-discipline that is a must for staying within the guardrails.

Do your reps have the sensitivity to adapt their timing?

Appropriate Compensation

You must provide appropriate compensation for each inside sales rep, tied directly into their goal. The goal of each inside sales rep is to set quality appointments. As discussed earlier, a quality appointment is one that ultimately leads to sales.

You can compensate the inside sales reps in several ways:

- Pay by the hour
- Pay by salary
- Contribute a benefits package
- Extend commissions
- Offer limited incentives

For example, if an ISR has set a goal of ten quality appointments per month and they meet that goal, they receive their set amount of compensation. If they achieve appointments beyond their targeted number, then you can increase their compensation. But you need to keep it simple for each inside sales rep so they can figure out exactly how much money they could potentially make.

My suggestion would be to pay everyone equally because when everyone is paid equally, there's no jealousy. It promotes real teamwork because everyone knows they are on the same line. There are times you might want to do a seasonal promotional contest, such as during the winter holidays, which would allow anyone who achieves that goal to earn more money for holiday purchases. That's fine. The compensation should be adequate to cause them to reflect on their worth within your company — they should know that the compensation is a reflection of their value on the team.

INTANGIBLES

Some people hold qualities that can't be measured. As you consider the individual and their fitness for the position of ISR, you might appreciate certain intangibles — things that don't fit on a form. It may be what they do or don't do. It's something you can't put your finger on or a dollar figure on, but it's within the makeup of their whole job description. It's what they bring to the table. It's what they bring to work every day. It's their personality. These qualities include accountability, proactivity, and creativity.

Accountability

The inside sales rep needs to take the position of owning their own business. This is true accountability. The principles of the ISR are the same as a business owner would have. For instance, *showing up*. That doesn't mean just being on time, but it means that they come through the door with their whole self, ready to work. They are mentally ready to meet the tasks required for their job.

They should recognize their areas of need and be *willing to ask for help*. This means that either they need a coach or training, or the company needs to help educate them. The inside sales rep needs to be self-aware of needing additional help.

Above all, they need to be *accountable for their own number*. They need to make the number, come hell or high water, in any situation from high to low. There is no excuse. They won't blame a lack of appointments on the script, the timing, or the weather. It all boils down to the numbers they call, the conversations they have, and the number of appointments they set. We will discuss that breakdown later in the chapter. Every individual must be accountable as though they own and run their own business.

Proactivity

I use *proactive* to mean anything the ISR does to improve themselves and their performance before something goes wrong or before they are confronted by management for lack of production. I was talking earlier about self-awareness. The inside sales rep must be so self-aware that they will take the proactive steps of asking for training and looking for any type of training programs. They work longer hours. They come in earlier. They work through lunch. They work past closing. They do anything that needs to be done in anticipation of meeting their target.

Joining chat groups is a proactive step, for example. When they join a chat group with their peers, they ask questions and gain the experience of individuals like themselves. They ascertain ideas, talk through issues, and gain different perspectives of how they can exceed expectations in their business.

Another proactive step is listening to training material or motivational tapes outside of work, whether driving in the car or working out in the gym. Our technology today is such that you can download books, videos, or anything else to your cell phone. With this type of technology, the rep capitalizes on the benefits of constantly having access to those resources and improving their skillset.

A proactive sales rep is coachable. They are willing to learn new ideas. They are willing to turn corners, and they are willing to break out of their own box to do well. They are always looking for ways to better themselves. They don't settle for the plateau, or their sales, like the land, will be flat. Proactive ISRs are always searching for the next mountain to climb. The inside sales rep needs to have proactive ideas.

Another way to encourage your ISRs to be proactive is to suggest they join a professional association, such as the American Association of Inside Sales Professionals. The AAISP is based in Minneapolis and runs an accredited school where they can take classes. They put on a conference once or twice a year. Regional groups of the AAISP can join to meet regularly. Paying dues and joining an organization offers the ISR yet one more way of connecting and learning more, improving their skills.

Creativity

In order to stay in contact with a prospect, the ISR must sometimes be creative. We discussed the importance of scripts and how they need to be followed, but sometimes the prospect will throw the rep a curveball or say something that will distract them. At that time, the rep needs to be creative and come up with a way of doing a workaround.

When I get a cold call from an inside sales rep, I purposely interject a comment, just to see if I can take the rep off their script. Maybe this is mean, but I am more interested in the skillset of the rep who is calling me. It's like a learning process for me — part of my research.

After they've asked my name and tell me theirs and their company's name, without a beat, I say something like, "Oh yeah, that's right. You never sent me the flowers you promised me during your last call."

And then I pause. If the rep skips over my comment, I can tell that they are reading a script, which tells me that they are not really listening to me. Therefore, I am just being pigeonholed into what their discussion would be rather than around my particular needs.

If the sales rep laughs or comes back to me with any type of comment that tells me that they heard me, I decide that this is a rep I want to speak with because they are interested in me as a person.

I understand that inside sales reps do have a script they need to follow, like I have mentioned. They need to stay within the guidelines of a script like a car is confined by a guardrail. But as a professional, even though I know there is a script, I enjoy talking with the inside sales rep because I want to see if they are a true professional.

When the inside sales rep develops creative ways to keep the prospect engaged, they are really building the relationship.

If the prospect says, "I can't talk to you now. I need to take my dog to the vet."

As an inside sales rep, my response might be, "Oh, I'm sorry. What kind of dog do you have?"

That is a question that every dog owner is proud to tell you, what type of dog they own. Once they tell you, say, "Okay, great. Good luck. I will call you later."

When the rep speaks to the prospect in the next conversation, they should ask:

It's, "How is your dog? Last time we spoke, you had to take him to the vet. Is everything okay?"

Pause.

The relationship is started, trust is being built, and the communication and conversations will become easier and easier and easier.

The ultimate goal of an inside sales rep is for the prospect to see the caller ID and pick up because it's the rep's name or their company's name. This is the ultimate success for each inside sales rep.

The inside sales rep should also be looking for that one more piece of information so they can add it to the CRM. If they gather one more piece of information by being a little bit creative, it just adds another arrow into their quiver. Arrows in a quiver is an analogy which means the rep can reach back and pull any type of information — the arrow — that is needed to keep the prospect on the phone longer and build a stronger conversation. Over a period of time, the percentage of prospects who have a number of quality conversations will lead into an appointment, and most likely, a sale in the end.

KEY PERFORMANCE INDICATORS

Key performance indicators (KPIs) are just that, the keys for your business to know what your projection is for inside sales reps, if they are meeting your expectations.

There are four major key performance indicators to know if your inside rep is successful:

1. Dials made
2. Conversations had

3. Appointments set
4. New contracts signed

Success relies on these four numbers. Chart them, review them weekly, review them monthly, and discuss them rather than the weather or trying to solve the problems of the professional football or basketball team. It's a conversation that needs to happen on a regular basis.

The question an executive needs to always ask their sales reps is: *Are you making your numbers?*

It's a mathematical equation really.

In order to explain the relationship of these four numbers, I have included a worksheet below:

KPI WORKSHEET

This worksheet is used to determine four important KPI numbers that measure the productivity of the ISR. By knowing these four numbers owners can manage their inside sales team and their company in an operational manner as they plan for future growth.

# of calls dialed/hour _____

# of hours/day _____

# of days/week _____

Total calls/week= _____

The call to conversation % _____

Total conversations/week= _____

% of conversations to appointments _____

**Total number of appointments
set/week=** _____

The outside sales rep
appointment to sale % _____

Total sales/week= _____

Average sales revenue= $ _____

Total week revenue= $ _____

Multiply by 52 weeks _____

Total year sales for the ISR = $ _____

Compensation of ISR = $ _____

ROI (Return on Investment) +/- _____

To Reach a Sales Target Increase

The KPI Worksheet is like a blueprint that can give you an immediate idea whether you have a successful or unsuccessful inside sales rep. This should be tied to their compensation.

The formula calculation below will also help you decide how many inside sales reps are needed to reach a sales target increase.

Sales dollar goal for the next 12 months $_____

(a)_____

The total year sales per ISR in your company

$_____(b)_____

The number of ISRs needed to meet the business target__(a divided by b)__

Now is decision time—you could:

1. Stay with your current position and do nothing

2. Hire additional ISRs, OR

3. Tweak the performance of the existing ISRs within the company

NOTE: Want to increase sales by double digits?

Option 3 is the best. Tweaking the number of dialed calls daily by the ISR leads to more conversations and appointments and increases the outside sales representative's closure rate. More sales will follow.

The Number of Dials

The dial or phone calls is the beginning of action. It's really the entry into the game.

The objective is for the ISR to introduce the company to the prospect, and then quickly decide yes or no: is the call worth the time to investigate further?

If it's a call that is not worth the time the rep needs to exit and move on to the next call.

The ISR can increase the number of calls by practicing the script and consulting it during the call. Their number of dials per day should match the company's expectations, which is part of the goal set on the worksheet. Emails or any other type of communication that are *not* dialing the prospect directly are *not* considered a dial. Emails are never considered to be phone calls.

The Number of Conversations

The objective of the conversation is to build a relationship with the prospect on the other side of the phone. A *conversation* is defined by getting the other individual, that prospect, on the other side of the line. This should not be just anyone within the company — the prospect needs to be a decision-maker, someone who can authorize purchases. That is considered a conversation.

Now, there are gatekeepers and assistants answering the phones. One of the reasons for a conversation is for the rep to listen, listen, listen for any type of helpful information that might lead them toward the next appointment. Although they are not the primary target for the ISR, gatekeepers and assistants may offer nuggets of information that can be added to the CRM and give the rep additional information for the next call. This is considered a conversation.

When an ISR is having a conversation, they need to be considerate of the prospect's time by making it a business call, not a social call. The prospect's time is too precious to have it be a social chat. Only if the prospect initiates a social comment should chatting be considered a gateway into a proper sales conversation. Then, the prospect has invited the rep in the door, so to speak. The ISR should never be the one to go knocking on the door to start a social conversation.

A successful rep always tries to get something in return for their call.

If the prospect says: *Call me next month,* the inside sales rep could say: *I'll do that, but when would be a good day or time?*

I have used the following comeback many times, and it's been very successful.

When the prospect says: *Can you call me back next month?* I'll say, *Thank you. I will. But seeing how you're busy, and I'm sure you're not wanting me to chase you or load your voice mail inbox with twenty different messages, what would be a good date and time that we could put on the calendar? I will then forward you a confirmed meeting notice to make sure nothing is scheduled over our call.*

Pause.

This question shows the prospect that the ISR is being considerate and respectful of their time. The rep in the meantime has gained a decision on the part of the prospect. This is a good time management procedure. The question exhibits professional behavior for the ISR which the decision-maker will recognize as respect for their time and establishes the ISR as a true sales professional in their mind.

If the potential client does not offer a specific call-back time, it probably means they were trying to give the rep the brush-off. If they had the opportunity to select a date and chose not to, the rep should move on because the prospect was not really interested in what the rep had to say.

The Number of Appointments Set

The objective of the inside sales rep is to set the appointment. This is the only number that matters in your KPIs. Without this number, nothing worthwhile has happened. In fact, Fred A. Perotta, leading salesman, trainer, consultant, and author, entitled his book, *Nothing Happens Until a Sale Is Made* (Booksurge Publishing, 2004).

If the rep can't make the appointment, the company won't be able to make the sale. The appointment is the precursor to the action of the sale. The number of appointments that needs to be set depends on other KPIs that a business owner might not know, but they can guess or have a good idea and then tweak the formula as needed.

Those numbers are:

- The number of appointments that need to be set, depending on the dollars
- The number of sales needed
- The amount of sales that are needed for that day, week, or month

Refer to the worksheet. It will show you, based on the amount of revenue that you want to generate within twelve months, the number of sales that you need to have. Using that worksheet, you can figure out the number of appointments that need to be set, the number of conversations necessary to set those appointments, and the number of dials made to have a certain amount of conversations that will ultimately lead to the sale. Remember, not every appointment leads directly into a sale.

There is another number you need to calculate, and that is the *closure rate of appointments*. This number is based on the industry and whether it is a multi-appointment sale or a one-close sale. You need to know what percentage of appointments lead to sales so that you know exactly how many appointments need to be scheduled on average for you to make that revenue number.

The measurement for determining the success of the inside sales rep is whether they are meeting goals and targets for dials, conversations, and appointments set.

In this formula, the business owner also needs to know the average dollar amount for the average sale. The owner needs to divide the revenue target price per sale into the number the owner wants to reach, which then gives the owner the number of sales for that particular period.

There is a caveat. Based on my experience, there is a limit to the number of dials the inside sales rep can physically make in an eight-hour day. Depending on the number of dials needed to make your sales goal per week or month, and how many calls can be made per rep in a day, you can figure out how many reps it will take to make the number goal.

Let's say your annual revenue goal is $100,000 for the company. Divide that number by 50, or the number of working weeks during the year, to see how much you need to make each week. In this example, that would be $2,000. Divide that by the average dollar amount per sale. In this particular case, if it's $500, you know the company needs to have 4 sales per week.

If your closure rate is only 25 percent, that means you need four times as many calls as appointments. Four multiplied by four is sixteen. So, you'll need to have at least sixteen appointments a week to yield four sales at $500 each, which is $2,000 a week, multiplied by fifty, to give you $100,000 at the top.

Next, you need to figure out what your *conversation-to-appointments-set* ratio is. If it is 10:1 or 10 percent — in other words, you make one appointment per ten calls — to set sixteen appointments, you need 160 conversations.

For this example, let's say your *conversation-to-dial* ratio is also only 1:10, 10 percent, or .10 (one tenth). To arrive at 160 conversations, there must be 1,600 dials.

Now, based on my research, most of the inside sales reps I spoke with said they can make twelve dials per hour. Multiply twelve calls per hour for an eight-hour day, and that's ninety-six dials per day, per rep. Now multiply by five days per week and you get 480.

So, to make 1,600 dials (your target number to yield 160 conversations on average) divided by 480 dials (the number of calls per week possible by one rep), you'd need precisely three full-time and one part-time inside sales team members.

Now, you have all the numbers you need to reach your target sales. If the numbers fall below the projected KPIs, take direct and decisive action. Falling behind and trying to make up time or number of dials or number of conversations is a hard and steep mountain to climb. If you have an inside sales rep who regularly does not tend to make their KPIs, you must determine whether that inside sales rep is a good fit for the company. Don't delay. All the evidence is there in black and white. You need to deal with the reality of a productivity problem when you see it.

CHAPTER FIVE

CHAPTER FIVE

What Is Needed for a Successful Inside Sales Department

YOUR RESPONSIBILITY AS AN EXECUTIVE

The process of creating an inside sales team will not be an instant profit maker. Hiring, training, purchasing working equipment, purchasing prospect lists and CRMS, and the cost of wages and benefits will make the startup seem like a heavy financial burden before any return on investment. It can be discouraging to read the first monthly financial statements, but the manager needs to be 100 percent dedicated and take an all-in approach. Their commitment must be shown as a first-class investment with a plan that they are devoted to following through.

Action is the key. The success of the inside sales team depends upon management to provide the right:

- Atmosphere

- Culture
- Personnel
- Technology

Management must also be patient with the process. Over time, the results and revenue will cover the expenses. But the key phrase here is *over time*.

How do you know if you're getting the return on investment you need?

You must review and tweak the process, which is typically done one step at a time. Each step and facet of training and setting up is examined to see whether it makes a positive difference. The manager is responsible for making sure the inside sales team has all the needed equipment and technology and that the process is well-defined.

Commitment to the Program

Every owner needs to be committed to the program because it will typically take longer than you'd think and probably cost more than you'd like to spend on it.

It may take as long as two weeks from the time you hire someone to the time they start their first day, then another four weeks for training, and yet another two to four weeks to work toward mastery of making calls. At that point, the rep is already eight to ten weeks into the process. They haven't even started producing revenue or appointments for you yet. This initial training time will always take longer than you think.

But you must be committed to the process and be willing to spend without the immediate return. Set a goal of one year before seeing appreciable results. Anyone can do anything for a year. In reality, plan to commit and invest in the program for up to a two-year period because that is when you start seeing the results.

Financially Supporting the Process

Committing to the process takes a lot of financial risk. You will have to spend the money before you see the return.

In addition to compensating your sales team members, there are other startup costs:

- Technical equipment
- The prospect list or CRM
- Physical office space

These are all costs to your overhead.

Understand as well that there's a bit of trial and error in hiring. It is known within the industry that for every two people you hire, one is either going to quit or you will need to terminate them. Unfortunately, this is also money spent upfront.

You need to have a marketing program that you financially support, which will hopefully help generate leads and dials for the inside sales team to make. You also have personnel issues — personal time off, family situations. That is another financial piece that is important but often not considered.

You must be willing to spend on marketing, technical equipment, and latest technology. You need to plan to hire good, competent inside salespeople, even if it is at a 50 percent rate. The bottom line is you need to figure out the expenses and figure out how long it will take to have a profitable and realized return on investment.

You might have to start out small. By starting out small, you gain small. Therefore, stretch. As you build, you will see the base build broader and the sales climb up higher. That is what you will want to have happen.

Another key financial piece you should strongly consider is hiring a competent sales coach who can handle and manage an inside sales team. This individual does not need to be hired as a W-2 employee. Most coaches I know work on a monthly or yearly agreement as a 1099 independent contractor.

Regular Review and Tweaking

There is a story of a gentleman who wanted to be a lumberjack. He took his axe and went to a logging camp up in the Northwest. The union guy hired him to cut down trees. He went out in the back field and cut down thirty trees on the first day. Chop, chop, they were just falling everywhere. The next day, he did the same thing, but this time, he was only able to chop down twenty-five. He was a little discouraged, but that's just the way it was. The next day, he went out and only chopped down twenty trees.

He had his axe dragging behind him on the way back to camp when his union manager asked, "Hey, what's wrong?"

The guy replied, "I wanted to be a lumberjack. The first time I went out there, I cut down thirty trees and thought that was what I was going to do daily. The second day, I only cut down twenty-five. The third day, only twenty. I just don't get it. I guess I'm not cut out to be a lumberjack."

The manager said, "Come here for a second." He brought the discouraged lumberjack over to the tool shed.

The lumberjack asked, "What is this?"

The boss said, "This is a sharpening tool, a grindstone. Put your axe on there and grind your axe."

Sharpening the axe needs to be approached with a sense of a commitment for your inside sales organization.

You must constantly measure the results of your inside sales team against the key performance indicators you have calculated. You need to have weekly meetings with your inside sales team to get input to see if they are dull, if they need their axes sharpened. You need to have an outside view, someone who can give an objective comment and look at the performance of the group, such as a sales coach.

In every quarter, you add or subtract something within the review or through the process to increase the performance and productivity. Another important factor is the script — also known as a sales premise.

Are the inside sales team members following the script?

You're looking for what is working and what is not. You are putting all the numbers onto a dashboard that you can view regularly to monitor activity. Then you can go back on a regular basis and not only review what the team has done, but you can tweak the process so it can be more successful and have more productivity for the next period, whether that be the next month or the next quarter.

HAVING THE PROPER TECHNOLOGY

When I was a small boy, I liked building with blocks. I would stack the individual blocks on top of each other until the stack would get so high, it would wobble and fall down. Eventually I got smarter, and I put two blocks on the base. With two blocks at the base, I could stack a little bit higher before the wobble and inevitable crash. I kept redesigning the base by putting more blocks next to each other. I built a broader base. I interlocked the blocks into a tighter fit. What I soon realized was that by increasing the base I could build a higher stack of blocks. Over time, with a base that was wide and supportive, I could create structures higher than I ever imagined.

I'd like to use this analogy to show that over time, the technology for the company is a broad base for the inside sales team. They must have the proper technology tools. The base must be solid. If the base is not solid in IT, everything falls apart, whether it be the CRM, prospect list, the equipment, or the structure itself. The building blocks of your technology should be widely and broadly built. You need to build a solid technology base so that the application tools you add to it are highly supported.

CRM

Your CRM (Customer Relations Management) is an important building block. This is the mechanism with which the rep or anyone having contact with your clients capture vital information that is used by the sales department as well as the marketing department. Typically, personal information is entered by the inside sales rep, but it can also be entered and sorted by your executives or a marketing executive if they are trying to do targeted marketing. A proper CRM also links into social media, but it's only as good as your input.

So, you need to tell your people to enter as much information as possible:

- Individual information
- Company information
- Notes from conversations
- Tasks

It should be easy for your people to extrapolate the information from the CRM to be used in different aspects of your company. When you provide a proper CRM, you are giving time and productivity back to the company by making sure all the information is put in one place in a timely fashion.

There are a number of CRMs on the market today. The best choice will depend on your specific need. Factors that will influence your decision are dependent on the type of IT technology already in place within the company and the technology that is supported.

The common items to consider within a CRM are:

1. Customer information
2. Contact information
3. List of accounts
4. Updated communication information
5. Compatibility of application software
6. Compatibility of social media networking
7. Leads and marketing programs
8. Mobile applications and functionality
9. Customization
10. Forecast measurements

It is difficult to compare the cost of CRMs because many factors, such as optional features and size discounting, vary from vendor to vendor. The best advice is to take the proper amount of time to arrive at the right decision for your company – don't rush the decision.

Auto Dialer and Dual Screens

When considering equipment for inside sales reps, more is better. Having two screens in front of an inside sales rep versus one makes a big difference. Here is why: the reps can use multiple screens to go from emails to social media networks, CRMs to a newsletter, from a blog sent to an individual to key information. They can toggle back and forth easily and efficiently on multiple screens. By doing such, the result is a better and more qualified lead.

It's also a part of making the inside sales rep feel like they are a part of the technology. You want to give them as much ease of use doing their job as you can. Their job is hard. Giving them the ease of going back and forth with information right at their fingertips is key. It makes them much more productive. Sometimes the inside sales rep is not recognized and respected as much as they should be. They will feel better supported and appreciated, and therefore be more productive, if you provide them the best technology for completing their job.

Where phones are concerned, you again want the greatest productivity possible. You don't want the inside sales rep manually dialing every call. An auto dialer, which prompts the next call with just a click on the phone icon, makes quite a significant difference in the number of calls that are made. Your reps can make up to ten phone calls more each day by using an auto dialer. Plus, an auto dialer moves the information seamlessly from one screen to another. It gives the inside sales rep an opportunity to fill in the information on one computer screen while the next call information is being populated on the second screen.

When you are talking about inside sales and generating leads, time is of the essence. The more time you give your inside sales reps to make appointments and make dials, the more appointments you will have.

Current Prospect List

A current prospect list can save you time and money. The information gathered and stored there must be correct. This is what makes it possible for the ISR to call the right individuals and the right companies at the right time.

By *prospect list,* I mean a list of information that goes into your CRM system. If Dan Fowler is listed as the CFO, but when the rep calls they find out that Dan is just in the accounting department, the rep has just lost valuable time. Your prospect list is only as good as the information is, and it must be up to date. Typically, you can buy these lists on a monthly basis. I know a lot of business owners who buy several at once. Unfortunately, they buy such a large number of names that by the time the ISRs get to them, the information is no longer reliable.

The prospect list can be categorized by industry. You can specify which *verticals,* or categories, you want to sort by. You may wish to sort by residential or commercial, whether the companies are tied to a specific geographical area, by potential services, such as manufacturing, distribution, attorneys, doctors, or any type of industry. You need to make sure your prospect list includes those vertical markets so that callers can make inquiries accordingly.

You want to find and focus on the sweet spot of your target market.

Here are some factors or items that you should have within a prospect list that should be current:

- Proper company names
- Executives' names
- Addresses of the headquarters and remote areas
- Correct phone numbers, extensions, and fax numbers
- Correct email addresses

Add to this list any other information you need to generate leads for businesses you will be selling to. That is the type of current prospect list you need to purchase.

GETTING THE SUPPORT YOU NEED

The inside sales team needs to have continual support. They have a job that no one in the company really wants. It's cold-calling—speaking with people you don't know, people who are rude, belligerent, angry, or will simply hang up on you in the middle of your introduction. It is not fun to deal with repeated rejection day after day, hour after hour, minute after minute.

Your operations team takes inbound calls, and your help desk takes inbound calls. They speak with people who really need to speak to the engineers of the company, and the business development and executive team work on appointments. Other people invite them into their circle or their company to speak with them. But that's not the same as what happens with the inside sales team. They are doing outbound appointment-setting. The inside sales team needs a moment of your encouragement, recognition of their tough job, and your praise and approval for a job well done. They need support from the company, and support from the industry personnel is necessary for their continuing success.

The key differentiator from an outside perspective for the ISRs is the guidance of a sales coach or sales mentor, someone who specializes within the inside sales work. Business owners, CEOs, and other executives take the time to have two or three different coaches direct them through their process or their company, maybe two or three coaching sessions a month. I have known executives who take four to eight hours of their time every month to work with a business coach to improve their own leadership and operational skills.

Doesn't it make sense to invest in a coach for one of the most important lead generating sales teams in your company?

Consider investing in four hours a month of coaching time for your inside sales team. They will thank you and it will give you, as the business owner or top executive, more time to concentrate on the main operations of the company.

Support From the Whole Organization

As I mentioned before, the inside sales job is a tough job to handle. If you took a poll about favorite jobs within the company, the inside sales team would not be the winner. You need to ensure the rest of the employees are not looking down on ISRs. Some folks mistakenly believe inside sales rep is an entry-level job — something anyone could do. It most certainly is not; the ISR is a professional and should be viewed as one.

Inside sales rep is a very tough job, and it requires a great deal of professionalism. Be sure to make your inside sales team part of your company's cultural events. Make them an integral part of the business and help the whole company realize they are an integral part of the business. ISRs are the entry, the first touch in many cases, of the business. If the inside sales reps are not achieving appointments, no sales can be made; no sales means the company does not produce a profit. Without profit, there can be no workers.

ISRs need to be regularly recognized, not only for the closed deals they have, but the appointments set and other accomplishments over a period of time. Your support can ensure the team stays positive, moves forward, and is regarded as an integral part of the whole organization, not the lowest rung on the ladder.

Support From the Industry

One of the strongest ways to keep the motivation, respect, and appreciation of the inside sales reps is to have a forum where they can regularly speak with their peers. This can alleviate a lot of stress as well, especially the pressure to stay professionally sharp all the time while they continually deal with rejection. As mentioned earlier, peer interactions are available via chat rooms, association memberships, and coachable groups. Time spent sharing their experiences with other inside sales reps is time your ISR can be transparent about their failures and successes.

With these kinds of connections, the ISR can learn from other ISRs. If they are currently making two appointments a week but are rubbing elbows with someone who makes four sales a week, they can find out, conversationally and in a low-stress environment, what the differences are between their performances.

It could prompt self-reflection for your ISR or a healthy sense of competition, to the point where they think: *If they can do it, I can do it too!* They may tell themselves: *I don't know how they do it, but I need to ask them what they are doing differently from me.*

It's a gauge that can be measured internally. The inside sales group as a whole can be that sharpening of the axe, that motivational spear that no one else within the organization can give.

The ISR many times feels alone in the job, and they basically feel like no one really understands what they're doing, their discouragements, or failures. A conversation with someone outside the company but in the same role can motivate and educate. The sales rep can learn their own process for becoming successful.

Support From an Outside Consultant or Coach

In theory, hiring a sales coach is not an expense to the company, but an investment that pays big dividends. From speaking with business owners, I found that many business owners really do not want to regulate or manage the inside sales team. They don't think they have the time or the energy for it. Although it is extremely important, they feel it is lower on the priority list. They would rather manage other higher priority issues such as making sure the operations team is functioning at peak efficiency.

Some of the owners I spoke with flat-out did not want to manage the ISRs. They felt they could not control the team and manage other parts of the company. They felt they did not have the time to manage the hiring, firing, training, and attend the weekly meetings that are necessary. Or, they would pick someone, typically an outside salesperson or a senior person on staff, and say: *You manage them.* My conclusion is that many business owners feel the inside sales team sucks so much of their time on a daily basis they are unable or want to deal with the inside sales issues or problems. This is where the coach is needed.

A coach hired specifically for the inside sales team can work in a timely way. The coach can hold weekly or monthly meetings on site or remotely. They can devote time to check in on a regular basis, maybe fifteen minutes at the end or beginning of the day, to answer any questions or monitor the inside sales team's activity.

They have immediate direct access to the inside sales team, whether the inside sales team is within an office or working remote. Even if the reps are working remote, the sales coach still has direct contact with them and can schedule regular appointments with them that will not be missed. The company executive might have a conflict in their schedule that either pushes the meeting to a later time or cancels the meeting. The coach can make it happen on a regular basis.

The sales coach takes the pressure and issues off the owner's plate. They can talk more honestly and be more objective with the sales team. ISRs can ask tougher questions of a sales coach, knowing that the sales coach will not become upset or take things personally the way an owner might.

Because their primary job is to focus on the sales team, a coach will show up reliably and be on time. An executive might have to deal with urgent matters that come up suddenly and need to change their schedule. A sales coach never cancels the appointment; they always hold it.

One of the biggest advantages an inside sales coach provides a business owner is collecting information from the inside sales team, summarizing it, categorizing it, putting some performance indicators to it, and generating a report that is best delivered to the business owner in a face-to-face meeting. If a sales coach does all the work behind the scenes and brings the results to the business owner, within one hour the business owner will understand the current status of the inside sales team.

When hiring a coach, you will need to have an agreement that not only states the length of the agreement and the payment, but the expectations of results the company is hoping to achieve. The coach helps align the business within the business's tactics and strategic guidance. This can all be done on a weekly or a bi-weekly basis, but I recommend that the coaching sessions are held with the ISRs at least every two weeks. If you wait a month between meetings, it could hinder motivation and the impact of coaching. Inside salespeople tend to wander, and like a herd of cats, the coach will need to gather the team back together again.

In the bigger picture, a sales coach is an excellent investment that in the end pays better than average dividends for the company.

I honestly believe that with support of the organization, support of the industry, and support of the sales coach, you can help your inside sales team achieve success sooner and with clearer focus. Those three qualities can produce results much quicker for your company.

Conclusion

Managing or establishing the inside sales team is a difficult task, a task not for the faint of heart. It takes dollars, hours, time, and patience.

My objective is to save you, the business owner, time and money by offering different ideas and steps toward experiencing a major revenue stream for any type of business. Although the procedure is hard, at the end of the process, it will be worth it. If you follow the steps that I outline in this book, you will grasp the concepts of what is needed and can use them as a guide to build your team.

Having read this book, you are ready to build your inside sales team. If you currently have a team, and it's not functioning well, this book will help you understand how to improve your business model to maximize greater revenue.

The best approach is to interview and hire an inside sales coach or consultant, one who has experience in building and managing sales teams. This will save you time — as the owner, you're probably not really focused on this avenue of the business; you are probably more focused on the amount of the company's revenues, not on the sales process. Your focus is most likely on the operations and making sure that customer support is intact, rather than the inside sales team.

There is an old saying in business: *Having a consultant does not cost, but it pays.* That has been proven. All the successful professional people—whether they are business owners or high-level executives or actors or athletes—have coaches and consultants.

Why would you not want a coach for your inside sales team?

Only by having a coach or consultant—a third party or outside perspective—work with the team can you be assured that there is someone who can talk objectively and honestly about what needs to be done for a successful team and raise the revenues of the company.

One final word: to reach the highest level of company sales, a second sales team—inside sales—which compliments the outside sales rep by setting quality appointments needs to be implemented. Following and measuring a defined process will produce the results you seek. If you do not have an inside sales team, my suggestion is to build one.

Good luck and good selling.

Next Steps

If, after reading this book, you would like to have a free, no-obligation consultation regarding improving the performance of your sales group, or if you would like to consider starting an inside sales team, please contact me directly. You may either email me at dan@danfowlerllc.com or call me directly on my cell: 630-240-5196.

We will discuss your goals, your expectations, and your timing. If there is a match in what we discuss, we will move forward by selecting a place and time to meet.

I am also available for motivational speaking engagements, for either large groups or smaller venues.

I look forward to having a meaningful dialogue with you soon.

Dan Fowler
Designing Strategic Growth

About the Author

Dan Fowler is a sales executive, small to medium business sales consultant, and an executive coach.

Dan is currently a Director of Business Development for an IT company. Having been in the IT industry for more than twenty-five years, he has worked for the largest of companies—such as Siemens and Lucent Technologies—and the smallest of start-ups that have gone public. His sales training is world class, including learning sophisticated and complex solutions for difficult problems. His high value of education has led Dan to seek and obtain his certification as a business coach and consultant as an additional resource for his company and sales prospects.

Dan attended Olivet Nazarene University and earned a degree in business, with a minor in economics and psychology. For playing baseball and leading the basketball team to a national championship, he was elected to the University's Athletic Hall of Fame. During his four years at Olivet, Dan learned the importance of teamwork, leadership, and dedication that has translated to a successful career both individually and for others.

Dan has coached executives at all levels and consulted business owners on improving their business revenue. As a facilitator with a peer mastermind group in Chicago, Dan led an executive and business owner group for four hours per month in a program designed to elevate their business processes while challenging their existing ones. Dan is also currently coaching and working with the executives of a Chicago based not-for-profit organization of which he is proud to serve.

Dan has been described by his co-workers as one who is continually encouraging others. Always striving to be of service to people, he is constantly challenging individuals to break out of their mold of acceptance and reach their highest potential in life. Very approachable and present, Dan builds relationships and trust in an incredibly short time.

To learn more regarding Dan's strengths and skills, visit his website at danfowlerllc.com.